A FLASH OF FUCHSIA

Featuring the Patrizia Pouch in Stone (202) pattern on page 50

Clockwise from top right, featuring the Corrine Clutch in Slate (200) pattern on page 54, Yumiko Hat in Damson (233) pattern on page 34, Elika Wristwarmers in Ochre (240) and Cobalt (230) pattern on page 30, Patrizia Pouch in Dusk (220) pattern on page 50, Corrine Clutch in Damson (233) pattern on page 54, Ines Wristwarmers in Powder Blue (222) pattern on page 42 and the Patrizia Pouch in Teal (231) pattern on page 50

BRILLIANT BRIGHT COLOUR

Featuring the Ida Cowl in Cobalt (230) pattern on page 74

CONTENTS

INTRODUCTION

At MillaMia our ethos has always been about combining a love of knitting with a love of modern design. Naturally Soft Aran has been developed very much with this love of knitting in mind – the Aran weight lending itself to satisfyingly quick knits and a warm, chunky finish.

Featuring the Annette Scarf in
Teal (231) pattern on page 26

7

TO TOP IT ALL

Featuring the Yumiko Hat in Slate (200) pattern on page 34

If something is worth doing, it is worth doing properly.

The patterns in this book cover a full range of accessories. With over-sized enveloping snoods that will keep you warm and on trend, lots of wristwarmer designs that are great gift ideas, as well as a series of stunning bags that will amaze you with how sleek and sophisticated hand knitting can really be. There are patterns for what can be classed as a beginner knitter and also some more challenging stitches and shaping that will appeal to the more experienced.

A few new techniques might be needed to make the amazing bags and pouches within. To make sure you are fully supported in this we have included a series of 'how to' pictures and instructions, and as ever plenty of helpful hints and tips to guide you on your way.

We always feel that if something is worth doing, it is worth doing properly. That is why you will see in the photos of our samples of the Paola Tote that we have gone to the trouble of putting foot studs in the base of the bag. And why we bothered to line our bags with a nice bright contrasting lining. Nothing is complicated – it just requires a bit of patience and a leap of faith perhaps when trying something new. The results speak for themselves.

The patterns in this book range from the guilty pleasure of a one evening knit – for instance the Malin Hat, or the excitement of learning a new stitch technique that gives a fantastic finished effect – such as the Elika Wristwarmers. Colour (as with all MillaMia designs) is a key feature. A subtle toning colour change sometimes (as on the Bia Roll Edge Cowl), at other times a bold and striking colour clash (see the range of Elika Wristwarmers).

Whatever it is that inspires you to knit there will be something to motivate you to pick up your needles and start knitting.

YOU CAN NEVER HAVE TOO MANY BAGS

Featuring the Patrizia Pouch in Teal (231) pattern on page 50, the Corrine Clutch in Damson (233) and in Ochre (240) pattern on page 54

Top: Patrizia Pouch in
Teal (231) pattern on page 50

Bottom: Patrizia Pouch in
Dusk (220) pattern on page 50

A BAG FOR ALL REASONS

It's hard to believe these
stylish accessories are
hand knitted. The bags
can be used for a variety
of purposes - as a wallet,
for your keys or for your
jewellery.

Featuring the Corrine Clutch in Ochre (240) pattern on page 54

Featuring the Ines
Wristwarmers in Powder
Blue (222) pattern on
page 42

BASIC INFORMATION

SKILL LEVELS

Recognising that we are not all expert knitters we have graded each pattern in the book to allow you to gauge whether it is one that you feel confident to try. The grades are as follows:

Beginner: You have just picked up (or refound) knitting needles and are comfortable with the basic concepts of knitting. By reading carefully you can follow a pattern. Items such as scarves and blankets and simple jumpers are ideal for you to start with.

Beginner / Improving: Having knitted a few pieces you are now looking to try new things, for instance colour combinations and features such as pockets. You might surprise yourself by trying one of the simpler colourwork or cable patterns in this book – you will find that they are not as difficult as you may have thought. Bear in mind that most experienced knitters will be happy to help a beginner. Or look at our website for advice and help.

Improving: You have knitted a variety of items such as jumpers, cardigans and accessories in the past, and are comfortable with following patterns. You may have tried your hand at cable knitting and some form of colourwork before.

Experienced: You are comfortable with most knitting techniques. You have preferences and likes and dislikes, although are willing to try something new. You can read patterns quickly and are able to adapt them to your own requirements – for instance if resizing is needed.

YARN – SOME ADVICE

As there can be colour variations between dye lots when yarn is produced, we suggest that you buy all the yarn required for a project at the same time (with the same dye lot number) to ensure consistency of colour. The amount of yarn required for each pattern is based on average requirements meaning they are an approximate guide.

The designs in this book have been created specifically with a certain yarn composition in mind. The weight, quality, colours, comfort and finished knit effect of this yarn is ideally suited to these patterns. Substituting for another yarn may produce a garment that is different from the design and images in this book.

TENSION / GAUGE

A standard tension is given for all the patterns in this book. As the patterns are in different stitch types (e.g. stocking, garter, rib, etc.) this tension may vary between patterns, and so you must check your tension against the recommendation at the start of the pattern. As matching the tension affects the final shape and size of the item you are knitting it can have a significant impact if it is not matched. Ensuring that you are knitting to the correct tension will result in the beautiful shape and lines of the original designs being achieved.

To check your tension knit a square according to the tension note at the start of each pattern (casting on an additional 10 or more stitches and knitting 5 to 10 more rows than specified in the tension note). You should knit the tension square in the stitch given in the note (e.g. stocking, garter, moss, etc). Once knitted, mark out a 10cm by 10cm / 4in by 4in square using pins and count the number of stitches and rows contained within. If your tension does not quite match the one given try switching to either finer needles (if you have too few stitches in your square) or thicker needles (if you have too many stitches) until you reach the desired tension.

USEFUL RESOURCES

We believe that using quality trims with our knitwear gives the garments a professional finishing touch. Visit your local yarn/ haberdashery shop for these items and MillaMia yarn or visit www.millamia.com to order yarn directly or find local stockists.

LANGUAGE

This book has been written in UK English. However, where possible US terminology has also been included and we have provided a translation of the most common knitting terms that differ between US and UK knitting conventions on page 20. In addition all sizes and measurements are given in both centimetres and inches throughout. Remember that when a knitting pattern refers to the left and right sides of an item it is referring to the left or right side as worn, rather than as you are looking at it.

SIZES

Alongside the patterns in this book we give measurements for most of the items. When it comes to the length of some items - for instance scarves you can of course make longer or shorter as you see fit.

CARE OF YOUR ITEM

See the ball band of MillaMia Naturally Soft Aran for washing and pressing instructions. Make sure you reshape your garments while they are wet after washing, and dry flat.

CONFUSED WITH A PATTERN?

The first thing to do is to check the Hints and Tips section in the pattern. In this we include useful additional notes which may answer your query. Or look on our website under the 'Making Knitting Easy' section or our blog if it is a technique query you have.

We check every MillaMia pattern numerous times before we go to print. Despite this occasionally there can be errors in knitting patterns. If you see what you think is an error the best thing is to visit www.millamia.com where any errors that have been spotted will be published under 'Pattern Revisions'. If you cannot find the answer you are looking for, then do send an email (info@millamia.com) or contact us via the website and we will get back to you.

BAGS OF STYLE

Featuring the Paola Tote in Cinder (201) pattern on page 58

Featuring the Bia Roll Edge
Cowl in Stone (202) and Pink
Glaze (223) pattern on page 82

ABBREVIATIONS

alt	alternate
approx	approximately
beg	begin(ning)
cont	continue
dec	decrease(ing)
foll	following
g-st	garter stitch
inc	increase(ing)
k or K	knit
k2 tog	knit two stitches together
m1	make one stitch by picking up the loop lying before the next stitch and knitting into back of it
m1p	make one stitch by picking up the loop lying before the next stitch and purling into back of it
mths	months
p or P	purl
p2 tog	purl two stitches together
patt	pattern
psso	pass slipped stitch over
pwise	purlwise
rib2 tog	rib two stitches together according to rib pattern being followed
rem	remain(ing)
rep	repeat(ing)
skpo	slip one, knit one, pass slipped stitch over – one stitch decreased
sl	slip stitch
st(s)	stitch(es)
st st	stocking stitch
tbl	through back of loop
tog	together
yf	yarn forward
yo	yarn over
yon	yarn over needle to make a st
yrn	yarn round needle
y2rn	wrap the yarn two times around needle. On the following row work into each loop separately working tbl into second loop [ ] work instructions within brackets as many times as directed
ytb	yarn to back
ytf	yarn to front

UK AND US KNITTING TRANSLATIONS

UK	US
Cast off	Bind off
Colour	Color
Grey	Gray
Join	Sew
Moss stitch	Seed stitch
Tension	Gauge
Stocking stitch	Stockinette stitch
Yarn forward	Yarn over
Yarn over needle	Yarn over
Yarn round needle	Yarn over
y2rn	yo2

KNITTING NEEDLE CONVERSION CHART

Metric, mm	US size
2	0
2.25	1
2.5	1
2.75	2
3	2
3.25	3
3.5	4
3.75	5
4	6
4.25	6
4.5	7
5	8
5.5	9
6	10
6.5	10.5
7	10.5
7.5	11
8	11
9	13
10	15

Featuring the Annette Scarf in
Stone (202) pattern on page 26

Featuring the Bia Roll Edge
Cowl in Cobalt (230) pattern
on page 82

24

ANNETTE SCARF

SKILL LEVEL **Improving**

SIZES / MEASUREMENTS
Approx 24cm/9 ½in wide by 280cm/110in long excluding fringing.

MATERIALS
- 12 (plus one ball for fringing) 50g/1 ¾oz balls of MillaMia Naturally Soft Aran in Teal (231).
- Pair of 5mm (US 8) needles.
- Cable needle.
- Crochet hook.

TENSION / GAUGE
18 sts and 24 rows to 10cm/4in square over st st using 5mm (US 8) needles.

HINTS AND TIPS
This oversized scarf is a statement piece that will beautifully accessorise any winter coat. The scarf is knit in 2 pieces and then seamed in the middle to ensure that the cables always face in the same direction when the scarf is worn and to ease the weight on the needles while knitting. When preparing yarn for fringing, cut a piece of card 19cm/7 ½in wide. Wind the yarn, not too tightly, around the card. Press lightly with a damp cloth. Cut the yarn along one edge. Using a crochet hook, knot three lengths of yarn through each eyelet hole. Trim the ends so they are even.

ABBREVIATIONS
C12F, cable 12 front - slip next 6 sts on a cable needle and hold at front of work, k6, then k6 from cable needle.
C12B, cable 12 back - slip next 6 sts on a cable needle and hold at back of work, k6, then k6 from cable needle.
C6F, cable 6 front - slip next 3 sts on a cable needle and hold at front of work, k3, then k3 from cable needle.
C6B, cable 6 back - slip next 3 sts on a cable needle and hold at back of work, k3, then k3 from cable needle.
See also page 20.

SUGGESTED ALTERNATIVE COLOURWAYS

| Stone 202 | Damson 233 | Cobalt 230 | Latte 203 | Ivory 221 |

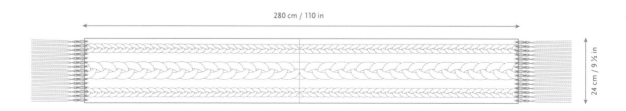

280 cm / 110 in

24 cm / 9 ½ in

TO MAKE

1st side

With 5mm (US 8) needles cast on 50 sts.

Eyelet row K2, [yf, k2 tog, k1] to end.

Next row P to end.

Next row P6, k2, m1, k3, m1, k2, p5, k2, [m1, k3] 4 times, p5, k2, m1, k3, m1, k2, p6. 58 sts.

Next row P to end.

Work in patt.

1st row P6, k9, p5, k18, p5, k9, p6.

2nd row P to end.

3rd row P6, k3, C6F, p5, k6, C12F, p5, k3, C6F, p6.

4th row P to end.

5th and 6th rows As 1st and 2nd rows.

7th row P6, C6B, k3, p5, k18, p5, C6B, k3, p6.

8th row P to end.

9th and 10th rows As 1st and 2nd rows.

11th row P6, k3, C6F, p5, C12B, k6, p5, k3, C6F, p6.

12th row P to end.

13th and 14th rows As 1st and 2nd rows.

15th row P6, C6B, k3, p5, k18, p5, C6B, k3, p6.

16th row P to end.

These 16 rows form the patt.

Cont in patt until scarf measures approx 138cm/54 ¼in, ending with a 2nd row.

Dec row P6, k3, slip next 3 sts on a cable needle and hold at front of work, k1, [slip 1 from cable needle, k next st from left hand needle, psso] twice, then k last st on cable needle, p5, k6, slip next 6 sts on a cable needle and hold at front of work, k2, [slip 1 from cable needle, k next st from left hand needle, psso] 4 times, then k last 2 sts on cable needle, p5, k3, slip next 3 sts on a cable needle and hold at front of work, k1, [slip 1 from cable needle, k next st from left hand needle, psso] twice, then k last st on cable needle, p6. 50 sts.

Next row P to end.

Next row P6, k7, p5, k14, p5, k7, p6 **.

Next row P to end.

Leave these sts on a holder.

2nd side

Work as given for 1st side to **.

TO MAKE UP

With both needles pointing in the same direction with right sides facing, knit one st from each piece together and cast off. For fringing see 'Hints and Tips' on previous page.

ELIKA WRISTWARMERS

SKILL LEVEL **Improving**

SIZES / MEASUREMENTS
Approx 18.5cm/7 ¼in long.

MATERIALS
• One 50g/1 ¾oz ball in each of MillaMia Naturally Soft Aran in Cinder (201) (A) and Emerald (241) (B).
• Pair each of 4mm (US 6) and 5mm (US 8) knitting needles.
• Cable needle.

TENSION / GAUGE
28 sts and 26 rows to 10cm/4in square over patt using 5mm (US 8) needles.

HINTS AND TIPS
These wristwarmers feature colour blocking and cables making them interesting to knit and cosy to wear. The pattern is unisex – have fun choosing cool colour combinations for every member of the family.

ABBREVIATIONS
C2F, cable 2 front - slip next st on a cable needle and hold at front of work, k1, then k1 from cable needle.
C2B, cable 2 back - slip next st on a cable needle and hold at back of work, k1, then k1 from cable needle.
See also page 20.

SUGGESTED ALTERNATIVE COLOURWAYS

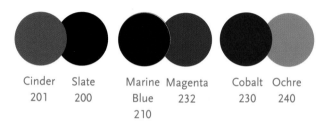

Cinder   Slate   Marine   Magenta   Cobalt   Ochre
201   200   Blue   232   230   240
                       210

18 ½ cm / 7 ¼ in

WRISTWARMER (make 2)

With 4mm (US 6) needles and A cast on 38 sts.
1st row K2, [p1, k2] to end.
2nd row P2, [k1, p2] to end.
These 2 rows form the rib.
Work a further 3 rows.
Inc row P2, [k1, m1, p2] to end. 50 sts.
Work in patt.
Change to 5mm (US 8) needles.
1st row (right side) K1, [C2F, C2B] to last st, k1.
2nd row K1, p to last st, k1.
3rd row K1, [C2B, C2F] to last st, k1.
4th row K1, p to last st, k1.
These 4 rows form the patt.
Cont in patt until piece measures 13cm/5 ¼in from cast on edge, ending with a 1st or 3rd row.
Cut off A.
Join on B.
Cont in patt until piece measures 17cm/6 ¾in from cast on edge, ending with a 3rd row.
Dec row P2, [p2 tog, p2] to end. 38 sts.
Change to 4mm (US 6) needles.
1st row K2, [p1, k2] to end.
2nd row P2, [k1, p2] to end.
These 2 rows form the rib.
Work a further row.
Cast off in rib.

TO MAKE UP

Join side seam, leaving an opening for the thumb.

YUMIKO HAT

SKILL LEVEL **Beginner / Improving**

SIZES / MEASUREMENTS
Approx 44cm/17 ½in in circumference, to fit an average adult head.

MATERIALS
• Two 50g/1 ¾oz balls of MillaMia Naturally Soft Aran in Damson (223).
• Pair of 5mm (US 8) knitting needles.

TENSION / GAUGE
18 sts and 24 rows to 10cm/4in over st st using 5mm (US 8) needles.
22 sts and 26 rows to 10cm/4in over patt using 5mm (US 8) needles.

HINTS AND TIPS
The pretty stitch pattern gives this hat lots of interesting texture and the rolled hem makes it an easy, comfortable fit. When adding your pompom to the top, go as large or as small as you are comfortable with (sample shown on the hat measures 8cm/3in in diameter). For perfect, fluffy pompoms every time, look in your local yarn shop or haberdashery store for a pompom maker, or buy a ready made pompom.

ABBREVIATIONS
See page 20.

SUGGESTED ALTERNATIVE COLOURWAYS

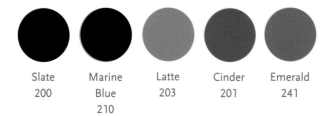

Slate 200

Marine Blue 210

Latte 203

Cinder 201

Emerald 241

22 cm / 8 ¾ in

TO MAKE

With 5mm (US 8) needles cast on 90 sts.

Beg with a k row work 7 rows in st st.

Inc row P2, [m1, p11] 8 times. 98 sts.

Work in patt.

1st row (right side) K1, [sl1pwise, k1, yrn, pass the slip st over the k1 and yrn] to last st, k1.

2nd row P to end.

3rd row K2, [sl1pwise, k1, yrn, pass the slip st over the k1 and yrn] to last 2 sts, k2.

4th row P to end.

These 4 rows form the patt.

Cont in patt until piece measures 18cm/7in from cast on edge, ending with a 4th row.

Shape crown

1st row (dec) K1, * sl1pwise, k3 tog, yrn, pass the slip st over the k3 tog and yrn, [sl1pwise, k1, yrn, pass the slip st over the k1 and yrn] twice; rep from * to last st, k1. 74 sts

2nd row P to end.

3rd row K2, [sl1pwise, k1, yrn, pass the slip st over the k1 and yrn] to last 2 sts, k2.

4th row P to end.

5th row (dec) K1, [sl1pwise, k1, yrn, pass the slip st over the k1 and yrn, sl1pwise, k3 tog, yrn, pass the slip st over the k3 tog and yrn] to last st, k1. 50 sts

6th row P to end.

7th row K2, [sl1pwise, k1, yrn, pass the slip st over the k1 and yrn] to last 2 sts, k2.

8th row P to end.

9th row (dec) K1, [sl1pwise, k3 tog, yrn, pass the slip st over the k3 tog and yrn] to last st, k1. 26 sts

10th row P to end.

11th row K2, [sl1pwise, k1, yrn, pass the slip st over the k1 and yrn] to last 2 sts, k2.

12th row P1, [p2 tog] to last st, p1. 14 sts.

Break off yarn, thread through rem sts and fasten off.

Join seam, reversing seam on st st section.

Make (or buy) a large pompon and attach to top of hat.

TILDA WRAP SNOOD

SKILL LEVEL **Improving**

SIZES / MEASUREMENTS
Approx 140cm/55in in circumference.

MATERIALS
- Five 50g/ 1 ¾oz balls of MillaMia Naturally Soft Aran in Dusk (220).
- Pair of 5mm (US 8) knitting needles.
- Cable needle.

TENSION / GAUGE
18 sts and 24 rows to 10cm/4in square over st st using 5mm (US 8) needles.

HINTS AND TIPS
An oversized wrap that looks luxurious and warm, the Tilda is perfect for accessorising a dark winter coat. Wear it long or wrapped double for two different looks.

ABBREVIATIONS
C6B, cable 6 back - slip next 3 sts on a cable needle and hold at back of work, k3, then k3 from cable needle.
T4F, twist 4 front - slip next 3 sts on a cable needle and hold at front of work, p1, then k3 from cable needle.
T4B, twist 4 back - slip next st on a cable needle and hold at back of work, k3, then p1 from cable needle.
See also page 20.

SUGGESTED ALTERNATIVE COLOURWAYS

Damson 233   Ivory 221   Cherry Red 242   Latte 203   Cinder 201

70 cm / 27 ½in

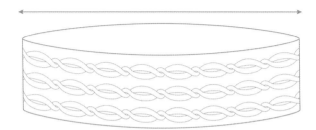

TO MAKE

With 5mm (US 8) needles cast on 48 sts.

1st row K4, [p4, k3, p2, k3] 3 times, p4, k4.

2nd row P4, [k4, p3, k2, p3] 3 times, k4, p4.

3rd row K4, p4, T4F, T4B, p4, k3, p2, k3, p4, T4F, T4B, p4, k4.

4th row P4, k5, p6, k5, p3, k2, p3, k5, p6, k5, p4.

5th row K4, p5, C6B, p5, k3, p2, k3, p5, C6B, p5, k4.

6th row P4, k5, p6, k5, p3, k2, p3, k5, p6, k5, p4.

7th row K4, p5, k6, p5, k3, p2, k3, p5, k6, p5, k4.

8th and 9th rows As 4th and 5th rows.

10th row As 4th row.

11th row K4, p4, T4B, T4F, p4, k3, p2, k3, p4, T4B, T4F, p4, k4.

12th row P4, [k4, p3, k2, p3] 3 times, k4, p4.

13th row K4, [p4, k3, p2, k3] 3 times, p4, k4.

14th row P4, [k4, p3, k2, p3] 3 times, k4, p4.

15th row K4, p4, k3, p2, k3, p4, T4F, T4B, p4, k3, p2, k3, p4, k4.

16th row P4, k4, p3, k2, p3, k5, p6, k5, p3, k2, p3, k4, p4.

17th row K4, p4, k3, p2, k3, p5, C6B, p5, k3, p2, k3, p4, k4.

18th row P4, k4, p3, k2, p3, k5, p6, k5, p3, k2, p3, k4, p4.

19th row K4, p4, k3, p2, k3, p5, k6, p5, k3, p2, k3, p4, k4.

20th and 21st rows As 16th and 17th rows.

22nd row As 16th row.

23rd row K4, p4, k3, p2, k3, p4, T4B, T4F, p4, k3, p2, k3, p4, k4.

24th row P4, [k4, p3, k2, p3] 3 times, k4, p4.

25th row K4, [p4, k3, p2, k3] 3 times, p4, k4.

26th row P4, [k4, p3, k2, p3] 3 times, k4, p4.

These 26 rows form the patt.

Work straight until piece measures 140cm/55in from cast on edge, ending with a 24th row.

Cast off in patt.

Join cast on edge to cast off edge.

INES WRISTWARMERS

SKILL LEVEL **Beginner / Improving**

SIZES / MEASUREMENTS
Approx 25cm/10in long.

MATERIALS
- Two 50g/1 ¾oz balls of MillaMia Naturally Soft Aran in Powder Blue (222).
- Pair each of 4.5mm (US 7) and 5mm (US 8) knitting needles.
- Cable needle.

TENSION / GAUGE
18 sts and 24 rows to 10cm/4in square over st st using 5mm (US 8) needles.

HINTS AND TIPS
These wristwarmers are a great introduction to cable knitting for an improving knitter who wants to try something a little more challenging. Each wristwarmer is a simple rectangle which is then seamed leaving a small hole for the thumb, which allows the knitter to concentrate on creating beautiful cables rather than shaping. A small, easily achievable project which makes a really thoughtful gift for Christmas or birthdays too.

ABBREVIATIONS
C4F, cable 4 front - slip next 2 sts on a cable needle and hold at front of work, k2, then k2 from cable needle.
C4B, cable 4 back - slip next 2 sts on a cable needle and hold at back of work, k2, then k2 from cable needle.
See also page 20.

SUGGESTED ALTERNATIVE COLOURWAYS

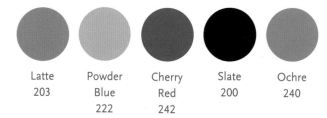

Latte 203 Powder Blue 222 Cherry Red 242 Slate 200 Ochre 240

25 cm / 10 in

RIGHT WRISTWARMER

With 4.5mm (US 7) needles cast on 53 sts.
1st row P2, [k1, p2] to end.
2nd row K2, [p1, k2] to end.
Rep these 2 rows twice more.
Change to 5mm (US 8) needles and patt.
1st row (right side) P2, [k1, p2] 11 times, k2, [C4F] twice, [p2, k1] twice, p2.
2nd row K2, [p1, k2] twice, p10, [k2, p1] 11 times, k2.
3rd row P2, [k1, p2] 11 times, [C4B] twice, k2, [p2, k1] twice, p2.
4th row K2, [p1, k2] twice, p10, [k2, p1] 11 times, k2.
These 4 rows form the patt.
Cont in patt until work measures 17cm/6 ¾in from cast on edge, ending with a wrong side row.
Thumb opening
1st row P1, patt to last st, p1.
2nd row P1, k1, [p1, k2] twice, p10, [k2, p1] 11 times, k1, p1.
These 2 rows form patt with g-st edging.
Work a further 16 rows.
Change to 4.5mm (US 7) needles for top of hand.
1st row P2, [k1, p2] to end.
2nd row K2, [p1, k2] to end.
Rep the last 2 rows once more and then the 1st row again.
Cast off in rib.
Join side seam, leaving opening for thumb.

LEFT WRISTWARMER

With 4.5mm (US 7) needles cast on 53 sts.
1st row P2, [k1, p2] to end.
2nd row K2, [p1, k2] to end.
Rep these 2 rows twice more.
Change to 5mm (US 8) needles and patt.
1st row (right side) P2, [k1, p2] twice, k2, [C4F] twice, [p2, k1] 11 times, p2.
2nd row K2, [p1, k2] 11 times, p10, [k2, p1] twice, k2.
3rd row P2, [k1, p2] twice, [C4B] twice, k2, [p2, k1] 11 times, p2.
4th row K2, [p1, k2] 11 times, p10, [k2, p1] twice, k2.
These 4 rows form the patt.
Cont in patt until work measures 17cm/6 ¾in from cast on edge, ending with a wrong side row.
Thumb opening
1st row P1, patt to last st, p1.
2nd row P1, k1, [p1, k2] 11 times, p10, [k2, p1] twice, k1, p1.
These 2 rows form patt with g-st edging.
Work a further 16 rows.
Change to 4.5mm (US 7) needles for top of hand.
1st row P2, [k1, p2] to end.
2nd row K2, [p1, k2] to end.
Rep the last 2 rows once more and then the 1st row again.
Cast off in rib.
Join side seam, leaving opening for thumb.

PONTUS PENCIL CASE

SKILL LEVEL **Improving**

SIZES / MEASUREMENTS
Approx 20cm/8in wide by 8cm/3in deep.

MATERIALS
• One 50g/1 ¾oz ball of MillaMia Naturally Soft Aran in Magenta (232).
• Pair of 4mm (US 6) needles.
• 35cm/14in zip fastener.
• *Optional:* Lining fabric 30cm/12in square.

TENSION / GAUGE
24 sts and 36 rows to 10cm/4in square over patt using 4mm (US 6) needles.

HINTS AND TIPS
As with all of these structured accessories the stitch pattern here creates a fairly dense fabric which lends stability and rigidity. Take time to insert the zip, handstitching in place to ensure a neat, working closure. This stitch produces a lovely texture so choose which side you prefer.

ABBREVIATIONS
See page 20.

SUGGESTED ALTERNATIVE COLOURWAYS

Cinder 201 Emerald 241 Cobalt 230 Stone 202 Cherry Red 242

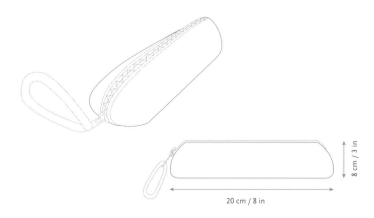

20 cm / 8 in

8 cm / 3 in

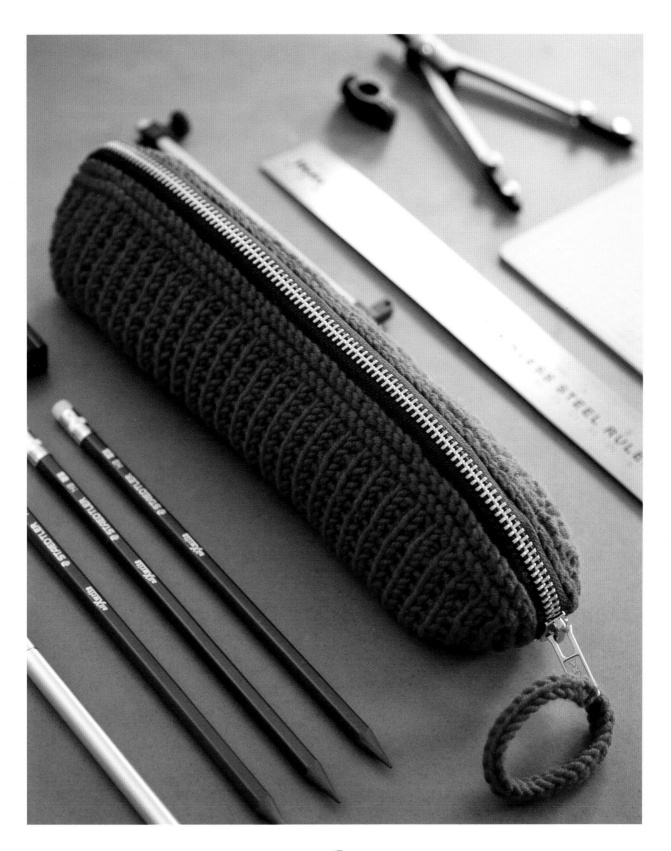

TO MAKE

1st side

With 4mm (US 6) needles cast on 51 sts.
** **1st row** P1, [k1tbl, p1] to end.
2nd row K to end.
These 2 rows form the patt.
Work a further 6 rows.

Shape sides

1st row Cast on 6 sts, p1, [k1tbl, p1] to end.
2nd row Cast on 6 sts, k to end. 63 sts.
Work a further 10 rows.

Shape top

Next 2 rows Patt to last 3 sts, turn.
Next 2 rows Patt to last 6 sts, turn.
Next 2 rows Patt to last 9 sts, turn.
Next row Patt to end.
Break off yarn, slip sts onto other needle.

Edging

With right side facing, using 4mm (US 6) needles, pick up and k9 sts along side edge, k2 tog, k59, skpo, pick up and k9 sts along side edge.
K 2 rows.
Cast off.

2nd side

With 4mm (US 6) needles, pick up and k51 sts along cast on edge.
K 1 row.
Work as given for 1st side from ** to end.

HANDLE

With 4mm (US 6) needles cast on 32 sts using the cable cast on method.
K 1 row.
Cast off.

TO MAKE UP

Stitch the base seam together first to create the pencil case shape. Pin your zip tape in place and then handstitch in place using stab stitch. If the zip tape is too long, the excess can be tucked inside for a neat finish. Thread ends of handle through zip pull and secure.

Optional Lining

If you wish to line your pencil case, please see 'Lining your knitted case' (page 86) for step by step instructions.

PATRIZIA POUCH

SKILL LEVEL **Beginner / Improving**

SIZES / MEASUREMENTS
Approx 20cm/8in wide by 13cm/5in deep.

MATERIALS
• One 50g/1 ¾oz ball of MillaMia Naturally Soft Aran in Dusk (220).
• 20cm/8in zip fastener.
• Pair each of 4mm (US 6) and 4.5mm (US 7) needles.
• *Optional:* Lining fabric 30cm/12in square.

TENSION / GAUGE
24 sts and 28 rows to 10cm/4in over patt using 4.5mm (US 7) needles.

HINTS AND TIPS
The pouch shape is made by knitting 1 rectangle, picking up stitches from the cast on edge and then knitting up a second rectangle. Thread a small piece of ribbon through the zip (as we have done in our photographed samples) if you want an easy, elegant zip pull.

ABBREVIATIONS
See page 20.

SUGGESTED ALTERNATIVE COLOURWAYS

| Stone 202 | Cobalt 230 | Pink Glaze 223 | Emerald 241 | Magenta 232 |

20 cm / 8 in

13 cm / 5 in

TO MAKE

1st side

With 4.5mm (US 7) needles cast on 50 sts.

P 1 row.

Work in patt.

1st row (right side) K1, [sl1pwise, k1, yrn, pass the slip st over the k1 and yrn] to last st, k1.

2nd row P to end.

3rd row K2, [sl1pwise, k1, yrn, pass the slip st over the k1 and yrn] to last 2 sts, k2.

4th row P to end.

These 4 rows form the patt.

Cont in patt until piece measures 12cm/4 ¾in from cast on edge, ending with a 1st or 3rd row.

Change to 4mm (US 6) needles.

Dec row P2, [p2 tog, p2] to end. 38 sts.

P 2 rows.

Cast off pwise.

2nd side

With 4.5mm (US 7) needles, pick up and k50 sts along cast on edge.

P 1 row.

Work in patt.

1st row (right side) K2, [sl1pwise, k1, yrn, pass the slip st over the k1 and yrn] to last 2 sts, k2.

2nd row P to end.

3rd row K1, [sl1pwise, k1, yrn, pass the slip st over the k1 and yrn] to last st, k1.

4th row P to end.

These 4 rows form the patt.

Cont in patt until piece measures 12cm/4 ¾in from cast on edge, ending with a 1st or 3rd row.

Change to 4mm (US 6) needles.

Dec row P2, [p2 tog, p2] to end. 38 sts.

P 2 rows.

Cast off pwise.

TO MAKE UP

Stitch the side seams together first to create the pouch shape. Pin your zip tape in place and then handstitch in place using stab stitch. If the zip tape is too long, the excess can be tucked inside for a neat finish.

Optional Lining

If you wish to line your pouch, please see 'Lining your knitted case' (page 86) for step by step instructions.

CORRINE CLUTCH

SKILL LEVEL **Beginner / Improving**

SIZES / MEASUREMENTS
Approx 30cm/12in wide by 20cm/8in deep.

MATERIALS
- Three 50g/1 ¾oz balls of MillaMia Naturally Soft Aran in Ochre (240).
- 30cm/12in zip fastener.
- Pair each of 4mm (US 6) and 5mm (US 8) needles.
- *Optional*: Lining fabric 50cm/19 ½in square.

TENSION / GAUGE
18 sts and 24 rows to 10cm/4in square over st st using 5mm (US 8) needles.
25 sts and 50 rows to 10cm/4in square over patt using 5mm (US 8) needles.

HINTS AND TIPS
The stitch pattern creates a nice sturdy fabric that lends stability to this clutch bag, so don't be concerned if your fabric feels a little dense as you are knitting it. Add lining after seaming and hand stitch the zip in to ensure a neat closure.

ABBREVIATIONS
See page 20.

SUGGESTED ALTERNATIVE COLOURWAYS

Slate	Damson	Teal	Cobalt	Cherry Red
200	233	231	230	242

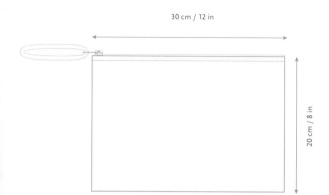

30 cm / 12 in

20 cm / 8 in

TO MAKE

1st side

With 5mm (US 8) needles cast on 57 sts.

** **Inc row** P3, [inc in next st, p2] 18 times. 75 sts.

Work in patt.

1st row (right side) K1, [sl1pwise, k1] to end.

2nd row K1, [ytf, sl1pwise, ytb, k1] to end.

3rd row K2, [sl1pwise, k1] to last st, k1.

4th row K2, [ytf, sl1pwise, ytb, k1] to last st, k1.

These 4 rows form the patt and are repeated throughout.

Cont in patt until piece measures 19cm/7 ½in from cast on edge, ending with a 1st or 3rd row.

Change to 4mm (US 6) needles.

Dec row K3, [k2 tog, k2] 18 times. 57 sts.

K 3 rows.

Cast off.

2nd side

With 5mm (US 8) needles, pick up and k57 sts along cast on edge.

Work as given for first side from ** to end.

HANDLE *(optional)*

With 4mm (US 6) needles cast on 80 sts using the cable cast on method.

K 1 row.

Cast off.

TO MAKE UP

Seam the sides using mattress stitch and then insert zip in the opening at the top, handstitching into place. Sew the handle in place on one side at the top as shown.

Optional Lining

If you wish to line your clutch, please see 'Lining your knitted case' (page 86) for step by step instructions.

PAOLA TOTE

SIZES / MEASUREMENTS

Approx 34cm/13 ½in wide by 24cm/9 ½in deep.

MATERIALS

- Seven 50g/1 ¾oz balls of MillaMia Naturally Soft Aran in Cinder (201).
- Pair each of 4mm (US 6) and 5mm (US 8) needles.
- 230cm/90in of 4cm/1 ½in wide webbing.
- *Optional:* 50cm/19 ¾in lining fabric.
- *Optional:* 100cm/39 ½in long by 15mm/1in wide ribbon.
- *Optional:* 4 foot studs.
- *Optional:* 35cm/14in by 20cm/8in piece of stiff card.

TENSION / GAUGE

18 sts and 24 rows to 10cm/4in square over st st using 5mm (US 8) needles.

25 sts and 50 rows to 10cm/4in square over patt using 5mm (US 8) needles.

HINTS AND TIPS

This classic tote is a stylish accessory with bags of appeal. It's capacious enough to hold all the essentials (including a knitting project!) and yet relatively compact when drawn in by the internal ribbons making it ideal for everyday use.

The knitting of this bag is actually very quick, but care and attention needs to be paid to the making up (as described in full details on pages 62-65) to ensure your finished item is as beautiful as it is practical.

ABBREVIATIONS

See page 20.

SUGGESTED ALTERNATIVE COLOURWAYS

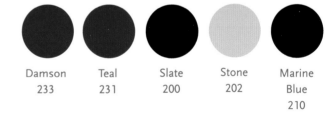

Damson	Teal	Slate	Stone	Marine Blue
233	231	200	202	210

20 cm / 8 in

34 cm / 13 ½ in

TO MAKE

1st side

With 5mm (US 8) needles cast on 64 sts.

** **Inc row** P1, [inc in next st, p2] 21 times. 85 sts.

Work in patt.

1st row (right side) K1, [sl1pwise, k1] to end.

2nd row K1, [ytf, sl1pwise, ytb, k1] to end.

3rd row K2, [sl1pwise, k1] to last st, k1.

4th row K2, [ytf, sl1pwise, ytb, k1] to last st, k1.

These 4 rows form the patt.

Work a further 20 rows.

Shape sides

1st row Cast on 10 sts, k1, [inc in next st, k2] 3 times across these 10 sts, patt to end.

2nd row Cast on 10 sts, p1, [inc in next st, p2] 3 times across these 10 sts, patt to last st, k1. 111 sts.

Beg with a first row, cont in patt until piece measures 24cm/9 ½in from side shaping, ending with a 3rd row.

Change to 4mm (US 6) needles.

Dec row K3, [k2 tog, k2] 27 times. 84 sts.

1st rib row P4, [k4, p4] to end.

2nd rib row K4, [p4, k4] to end.

Rep the last 2 rows twice more.

Cast off in rib.

2nd side

With 5mm (US 8) needles, pick up and k64 sts along cast on edge.

Work as given for first side from ** to end.

TO MAKE UP

See overleaf for step by step instructions for finishing the Paola Tote and insterting the optional lining.

STEP 1

Before seaming your knitted bag cut out the fabric for the lining using the knitted piece as a template. Fold fabric in half and lay folded knitted bag on top. Cut around allowing 1.5cm/½in for seam allowance on bottom and sides, and 2.5cm/1in along top edge.

STEP 2

Measure the distance between the indents (the 'L' shaped corners along the bottom of the piece) for the length of the base and the depth of the 'L's for the width. Cut a piece of stiff cardboard to fit the base.

STEP 3

Mark 4 positions for foot studs 2cm/¾in from the edges of the cardboard at all 4 corners and make a hole in preparation for later.

STEP 4

Sew the side seams of knitted bag together on the wrong side using an overcast stitch. Finish seam at point of indent (do not sew the 'L''s together flat.) At this point, to create width at the base pinch into a T shape and then finish sewing.

STEP 5

Attach webbing to the top edge using a sewing machine, or handstitch if you feel confident.

STEP 6

Cut webbing to 60cm/23½in for shoulder straps and place onto bag centred with 15cm/6in between the two straps. Sew into place using a 'box stitch' for a strong and secure handle.

STEP 7

Place card base into bag and insert foot studs 2cm/¾in from the corners of the bag and guide them through the precut hole in the board.

STEP 8

Open split pins on card side to secure them in place.

STEP 9
Insert all 4 before lining bag.

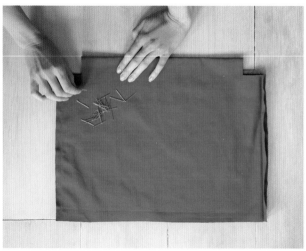

STEP 10
Pin lining right sides together, sew side seams together, stopping when you reach the 'L' shaped indent, and press side seams open so that they lay flat.

STEP 11
Sew the remaining base seam in a T-formation (see picture above) to finish the lining.

STEP 12
To fit the lining to the precise depth of your bag, drop lining into bag (wrong sides facing each other so that the right side of the lining is visible inside the bag), and at the appropriate height fold the top edge of the lining back on itself to create a neat folded top edge. Remove lining and press this fold with an iron.

STEP 13
Reinsert the lining and pin in place approx. 0.5cm/¼in from top edge of webbing and pin in place. Hand stitch to secure using a slip stitch.

STEP 14
Optional To create a more trapezoid shape for the Paola tote you can attach tabs of ribbon between the webbing and the lining by the side seams. Cut the ribbon in two 35cm/14in pieces, and handstitch in place.

STEP 15
The bag can be worn as a classic tote.

STEP 16
Or tie the ribbons together to draw the sides of the bag in creating a more closed trapezoid shape.

ASA
LONG WRISTWARMERS

SKILL LEVEL **Beginner**

SIZES / MEASUREMENTS
Approx 33cm/13in long.

MATERIALS
• Three 50g/1 ¾oz ball of MillaMia Naturally Soft Aran
  in Powder Blue (222).
• Pair of 5mm (US 8) knitting needles.

TENSION / GAUGE
18 sts and 24 rows to 10cm/4in square over st st using
5mm (US 8) needles.

HINTS AND TIPS
These cosy wristwarmers make an ideal first project for a
beginner. Knit entirely in rib with minimal shaping and only
one seam, they are a quick, achievable project that will ease the
beginner knitter into the rhythm of knitting and purling.

ABBREVIATIONS
See page 20.

SUGGESTED ALTERNATIVE COLOURWAYS

Latte
203

Cherry
Red
242

Teal
231

Pink Glaze
223

Magenta
232

33 cm / 13 in

WRISTWARMER (make 2)

With 5mm (US 8) needles cast on 50 sts.
1st row (right side) K2, [p2, k2] to end.
2nd row P2, [k2, p2] to end.
Rep these 2 rows until work measures 21cm/8 ¼in from cast on edge, ending with a 2nd row.
Dec row K2, [p2 tog, k2] to end. 38 sts.
Work 5 rows in rib as set, ending with a wrong side row.
Thumb opening
1st row K2, [p1, k2] to end.
2nd row K1, p1, [k1, p2] to last 3 sts, k1, p1, k1.
Rep the last 2 rows 5 times more.
Work in patt, for top of hand.
1st row K2, [p1, k2] to end.
2nd row P2, [k1, p2] to end.
Rep the last 2 rows 5 times more.
Cast off in rib.

TO MAKE UP

Join side seam, leaving opening for thumb.

GULLAN SNOOD

SKILL LEVEL **Beginner / Improving**

MEASUREMENTS

Approx 76cm/30in circumference by 44cm/17 ½in deep.

MATERIALS

- Seven 50g/1 ¾oz balls of MillaMia Naturally Soft Aran in Marine Blue (210).
- 5mm (US 8) circular needle.

TENSION / GAUGE

22 sts and 25 rows to 10cm/4in square over patt using 5mm (US 8) needles.

HINTS AND TIPS

The slipped stitch pattern here adds wonderful texture and is easily memorised after just a few repeats. We recommend using a circular needle working backwards and forwards to accommodate the large number of stitches and to help with managing the weight of the piece as it grows.

ABBREVIATIONS

See page 20.

NOTE

Take care not to pull the yarn tightly across the work when slipping stitches.

SUGGESTED ALTERNATIVE COLOURWAYS

| Cinder | Stone | Teal | Ivory | Damson |
| 201 | 202 | 231 | 221 | 233 |

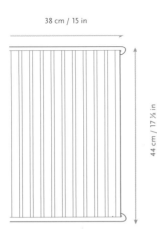

38 cm / 15 in

44 cm / 17 ½ in

TO MAKE

With 5mm (US 8) needles cast on 170 sts.

1st row (right side) P3, * [winding yarn around the needle twice, k1] 4 times, p4, rep from * ending last rep p3.

2nd row K3, * ytf, dropping extra loop, slip next 4 sts pwise, ytb, k4, rep from * ending last rep k3.

3rd row P3, * ytb, slip next 4 sts pwise, ytf, p4, rep from * ending last rep p3.

4th row K3, * ytf, slip next 4 sts pwise, ytb, k4, rep from * ending last rep k3.

These 4 rows form the patt and are repeated.

Work straight until piece measures 44cm/17 ½in, ending with a 4th row.

Next row P3, [k4, p4] to last 7 sts, k4, p3.

Cast off.

Join seam.

IDA COWL

SKILL LEVEL **Beginner / Improving**

SIZES / MEASUREMENTS
Approx 73cm/29in circumference by 31cm/12 ¼in deep.

MATERIALS
• Four 50g/1 ¾oz balls of MillaMia Naturally Soft Aran in Cobalt (230).
• 5mm (US 8) circular needle.

TENSION / GAUGE
18 sts and 24 rows to 10cm/4in square over st st and patt using 5mm (US 8) needles.

HINTS AND TIPS
When joining your work to knit in the round on a circular needle, take extra care to make sure that your knitting is not twisted. Once you have completed the first purl row, lay your knitting out on a flat surface and ensure that all stitches are laying in the same direction before commencing in the round. Also remember that garter stitch worked in the round is alternate rows of knit and purl.

ABBREVIATIONS
See page 20.

SUGGESTED ALTERNATIVE COLOURWAYS

Magenta 232   Cherry Red 242   Pink Glaze 223   Damson 233   Emerald 241

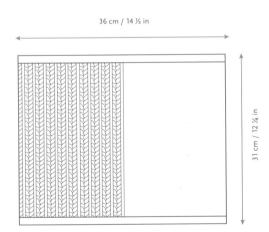

36 cm / 14 ½ in

31 cm / 12 ¼ in

TO MAKE

With 5mm (US 8) circular needle cast on 132 sts.

1st round P to end, join into a round.

2nd round K to end.

3rd round P to end.

Rep the last 2 rounds once.

Work in patt.

1st round K to end.

2nd round K66, [p1, k1] 33 times.

Rep the last 2 rounds until work measures 29cm/11 ½in from cast on edge, ending with a 2nd round.

Beg with a p round work 4 rounds in g-st.

Cast off pwise.

MALIN HAT

SKILL LEVEL **Beginner / Improving**

SIZES / MEASUREMENTS

Approx 44cm/17 ½in in circumference, to fit an average adult head.

MATERIALS

• Two 50g/1 ¾oz balls of MillaMia Naturally Soft Aran in Cinder (201) (A).
• Two 50g/1 ¾oz balls in Stone (202) (B).
• Pair each of 4.5mm (US 7) and 5mm (US 8) knitting needles.
• Cable needle.

TENSION / GAUGE

18 sts and 24 rows to 10cm/4in square over st st using 5mm (US 8) needles.
22 sts and 46 rows to 10cm/4in square over patt using 5mm (US 8) needles.

HINTS AND TIPS

This hat features colour blocking in 2 colours and a slip stitch pattern to add texture. A great opportunity to play with colour combinations to produce bold, subtle, colour clashing or tonal statements. Or, if you don't feel confident in selecting colour combinations of your own and would love to be brave then why not try our colour picking tool at www.millamia.com.

ABBREVIATIONS

See page 20.

SUGGESTED ALTERNATIVE COLOURWAYS

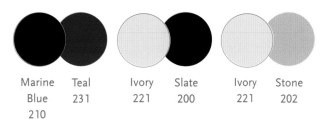

| Marine Blue 210 | Teal 231 | Ivory 221 | Slate 200 | Ivory 221 | Stone 202 |

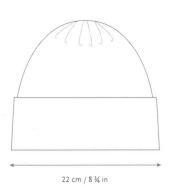

22 cm / 8 ¾ in

TO MAKE

With 5mm (US 8) needles and A cast on 98 sts.
1st row K to end.
2nd row K2, [sl2pwise, k1] to end.
Rep these 2 rows for 8cm/3in, ending with a 2nd row.
Mark each end of last row with a coloured thread.
Change to 4.5mm (US 7) needles.
Beg with a k row cont in st st.
Work 20 rows.
Cut off A.
Join on B.
Change to 5mm (US 8) needles.
Cont in st st until work measures 27cm/10 ½in from coloured
threads, ending with a p row.
Shape crown
Next row K1, * slip next 8 sts on cable needle and hold at
front of work, [sl next st on cable needle, k next st on left hand
needle, psso] 8 times, slip next 8 sts on cable needle and hold
at back of work, k next st on left hand needle tog with next st
on cable needle] 8 times, rep from * twice more, k1. 50 sts.
Next row P to end.
Next row K1, [k2 tog] to last st, k1. 26 sts.
Next row P to end.
Next row K1, [k2 tog] to last st, k1. 14 sts.
Break off yarn, thread through rem sts draw up tightly and join
seam.

BIA ROLL EDGE COWL

SKILL LEVEL **Beginner / Improving**

MEASUREMENTS
Approx 76cm/30in circumference by 57cm/22 ½in deep.

MATERIALS
Single colour version
- Nine 50g/1 ¾oz balls of MillaMia Naturally Soft Aran in Slate (200) or Cobalt (230) (A).

Two colour version
- Seven 50g/1 ¾oz balls of MillaMia Naturally Soft Aran in Stone (202) (A).
- Three balls in Pink Glaze (223) (B).

All versions
- Pair of long 5mm (US 8) needles or circular needle.

TENSION / GAUGE
19 sts and 40 rows to 10cm/4in square over patt using 5mm (US 8) needles.

HINTS AND TIPS
The Bia has been designed to be worn in 2 different ways, as a snood up over the head on chilly winter days or concertined around the neck as an oversized cowl. Either way it provides a generous accessory that will look stunning in one of our new bright shades or classic and cosy in a more muted melange.

ABBREVIATIONS
See page 20.

NOTE
Take care not to pull the yarn tightly across the work when slipping stitches.

SUGGESTED ALTERNATIVE COLOURWAYS

Stone 202
Cherry Red 242
Latte 203
Ivory 221
Marine Blue 210
Ochre 240

38 cm / 15in

57 cm / 22 ½ in

TO MAKE

With 5mm (US 8) needles and A cast on 144 sts.
Beg with a k row, work 6 rows in st st.
Cont in patt.
1st row (right side) K to end.
2nd row [K1, slip 1] to last 2 sts, k2.
3rd row K to end.
4th row K2, [slip 1, k1] to end.
These 4 rows form the patt and are repeated.
One colour version
Work straight until piece measures 56cm/22in, ending with a
4th row.
Two colour version
Work straight until piece measures 49cm/19 ¼in, ending with
a 4th row.
Cont in B, work straight until piece measures 56cm/22in,
ending with a 4th row.
All versions
Beg with a k row, work 6 rows in st st.
Cast off.

LINING YOUR KNITTED CASE

STEP 1

Before seaming your knitted case cut out the fabric for the lining using the knitted piece as a template. Fold fabric in half and lay knitted case (also folded in half) on top. Cut around allowing 1.5cm/½in for seam allowance on all sides.

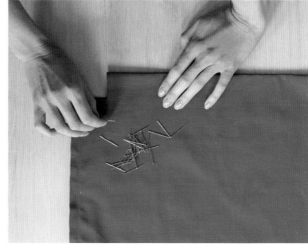

STEP 2

Pin lining right sides together, sew seams together (except for top edge), and press seams open so that they lay flat.

STEP 3

To fit the lining to the precise depth of your case, drop lining into the case (wrong sides facing each other so that the right side of the lining is visible inside the case), and at the appropriate height fold the top edge of the lining back on itself to create a neat folded top edge. Remove lining and press this fold with an iron.

STEP 4

Reinsert the lining and pin in place approx 0.5cm/¼in from the edge of the zip teeth and pin in place. Hand stitch to secure using a slip stitch.

YARN COLOURS

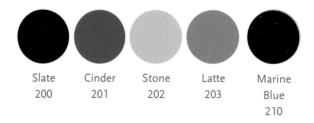

Slate
200

Cinder
201

Stone
202

Latte
203

Marine
Blue
210

Dusk
220

Ivory
221

Powder
Blue
222

Pink Glaze
223

Cobalt
230

Teal
231

Magenta
232

Damson
233

Ochre
240

Emerald
241

Cherry
Red
242

NOTES

INDEX

ANNETTE SCARF
page 26

ELIKA WRISTWARMERS
page 30

YUMIKO HAT
page 34

TILDA WRAP SNOOD
page 38

INES WRISTWARMERS
page 42

PONTUS PENCIL CASE
page 46

PATRIZIA POUCH
page 50

CORINNE CLUTCH
page 54

PAOLA TOTE
page 58

ASA LONG WRISTWARMERS
page 66

GULLAN SNOOD
page 70

IDA COWL
page 74

MALIN HAT
page 78

BIA ROLL EDGE COWL
page 82

FROM MILLAMIA

The last few months have been a mix of hard work and exhilaration as the whole MillaMia team has pulled together to prepare for the launch of our new yarn line Naturally Soft Aran. As this is only our second ever yarn range, it effectively equates to doubling our range. As when we started MillaMia with our original Naturally Soft Merino yarn, we wanted to make sure our Aran weight also enjoyed having two books of pattern support from the outset.

We quickly decided that a mix of both children and adult patterns would be appropriate, but wanted to keep them separate. We kept hearing that you loved knitting accessories, and so the idea of an entire book dedicated just to adult accessories was born.

And here it soon became apparent that Helena's day job in the luxury leather handbag world would be a real advantage for us. As part of testing the new yarn weight we did a lot of swatching in the office. Different stitch textures and combinations. Helena fell in love with the structure that certain stitch combinations in our new yarn produced and soon saw the potential for designing really beautiful, structured bags, pouches and cases. We are so pleased with the outcome. When you knit them, do take the time to follow our guide on how to line them if you want them to last you a very long time.

It would not be an accessories book without a few smaller, quick knits. The wristwarmers in this book are just that - quick, satisfying knits. We are particularly pleased with the Elika wristwarmers - combining the classic MillaMia play on colour with the fun of knitting a more unusual stitch pattern. The perfect gift for winter birthdays.

When it came to the photoshoot I have to confess to a moment of madness. At one point we seriously contemplated photographing both the children's and adult books on the same day. Thank goodness our model cancelled! In the end even the full day we spent capturing the wonderful images in this book was a stretch. We must thank our amazing photographer Emma, our hard working, beautiful model Cecile, and Katie (for make up) who made it all possible.

Finally we mentioned earlier that this was a team effort. It really has been. Maja has worked tirelessly in the office juggling scant yarn supplies (always the way with a new range before production has kicked in) and managing test knitters to allow us to show our items in all the glorious colour combinations you can see. Max has proofread and reviewed all the patterns before layout and as ever helped out in the lead up to the shoot with last minute finishing. Our new design intern Tanya has helped Helena from the outset with moodboards, managing colour swatches, set design and illustrations. One of our previous interns Louisa chipped in with her finishing skills. Kirsten as ever providing a boost of enthusiasm and strategic direction and encouragement at critical stages. This is our opportunity to say thank you to them all.

Thank you to you our customers also. Without your support and encouragement we may never have taken the leap to launch Naturally Soft Aran.

With best wishes,

Katarina and Helena Rosén
katarina@millamia.com or helena@millamia.com